Out and About at the Science Center

By Kitty Shea

Illustrated by Becky Shipe

Special thanks to our advisers for their expertise:

Dennis Schatz, Associate Director
Pacific Science Center, Seattle, Washington

Susan Kesselring, M.A., Literacy Educator
Rosemount-Apple Valley-Eagan (Minnesota) School District

PICTURE WINDOW BOOKS
Minneapolis, Minnesota

The author wishes to thank:

• Sarah Gardner and Dale Wiehle, Science Museum of Minnesota

• Sean Smith, Association of Science-Technology Centers Incorporated

Managing Editor: Bob Temple
Creative Director: Terri Foley
Editor: Peggy Henrikson
Editorial Adviser: Andrea Cascardi
Copy Editor: Laurie Kahn
Designer: John Moldstad
Page production: Picture Window Books
The illustrations in this book were prepared digitally.

Picture Window Books
5115 Excelsior Boulevard
Suite 232
Minneapolis, MN 55416
1-877-845-8392
www.picturewindowbooks.com

Printed in the United States of America.

Library of Congress Cataloging-in-Publication Data
Shea, Kitty.
Out and about at the Science Center / by Kitty Shea ; illustrated by
Becky Shipe.
p. cm. — (Field trips)
Includes bibliographical references and index.
Summary: Science center guide Maria gives a tour of the science center
explaining the various exhibits and activities that are found there and
the ways in which science centers differ from art and history museums.
Includes instructions for creating a science exhibit and other resources.
ISBN 1-4048-0297-5 (hardcover)
ISBN 1-4048-0202-9 (softcover)
1. Science centers—Juvenile literature. [1. Science centers. 2. Museums.]
I. Shipe, Becky, ill. II. Title. III. Field trips (Picture Window Books)
Q105.A1 S54 2004
507'.4—dc22
                                        2003016529

We're going on a field trip to the science center.
We can't wait!

Things to find out:

Is it okay to touch things here?

What exactly is science?

Where does a science center get all
of its stuff?

What kinds of things do scientists do?

Welcome to the science center! I'm Maria, and I'm going to show you around. Go ahead and touch anything that doesn't have a railing around it. Science is about touching and doing!

A science center is sometimes called a science museum. Many exhibits in a science center or museum are hands-on. That means visitors can touch and play with these objects and can do experiments. It's different at art and history museums. There, objects may be old, valuable, or easily damaged. Visitors may look but not touch.

5

Science is the study of something by testing, measuring, and doing experiments. All this studying is called research. Scientists study humans and other animals, plants, and Earth. They learn about natural forces, such as gravity and magnetism. They study the weather and objects in outer space. Scientists help people make amazing things, such as computers, medicine, and space shuttles.

Some science centers have scientists who help gather the objects and information on display. Centers might trade objects with other centers or museums. Sometimes people give centers their treasures. Exhibit builders take the objects and information and put together the displays. They might design and build totally new exhibits with the help of scientists.

7

Some scientists want to study old things, such as dinosaurs. This is our dinosaur, Diplodocus. Isn't he awesome? The last dinosaurs disappeared from the earth about 65 million years ago. Our friend here is much, much older than grandmas and grandpas—and a whole lot bigger!

Fossils are very old, hardened remains, such as bones, teeth, or claws. Fossils also might be footprints or other imprints in stone. Scientists take great care to uncover dinosaur fossils in the ground. This activity is called a fossil dig. Dinosaur fossils have been found throughout the world. In the United States, Diplodocus fossils have been found in Colorado, Montana, Utah, and Wyoming.

9

Some scientists want to study and help create new things. This is our Science of Sports area. Did you know that lots of science goes into making sports equipment and being a great athlete? In this area, you can safely try your skills in all kinds of sports. You can even design and test your own parachute, paper airplane, or roller coaster!

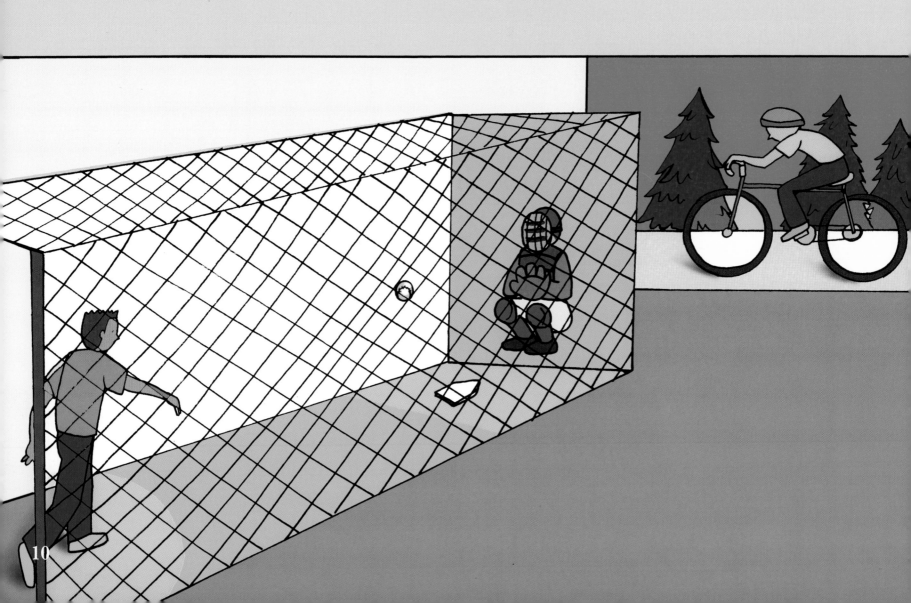

Sport scientists design sports equipment that is just the right size, shape, and weight. Good athletes use science to help them perform their sports better. For example, they might need to know the effects of gravity and wind. They also need to know how to use their muscles in the best ways.

11

It's your wonderful body that makes it possible for you to play sports—and do many other things. The human body includes much more than muscles and bones. We have a lot going on inside of us! Take a look through those microscopes. You'll be able to see tiny cells like the ones that make up our bodies.

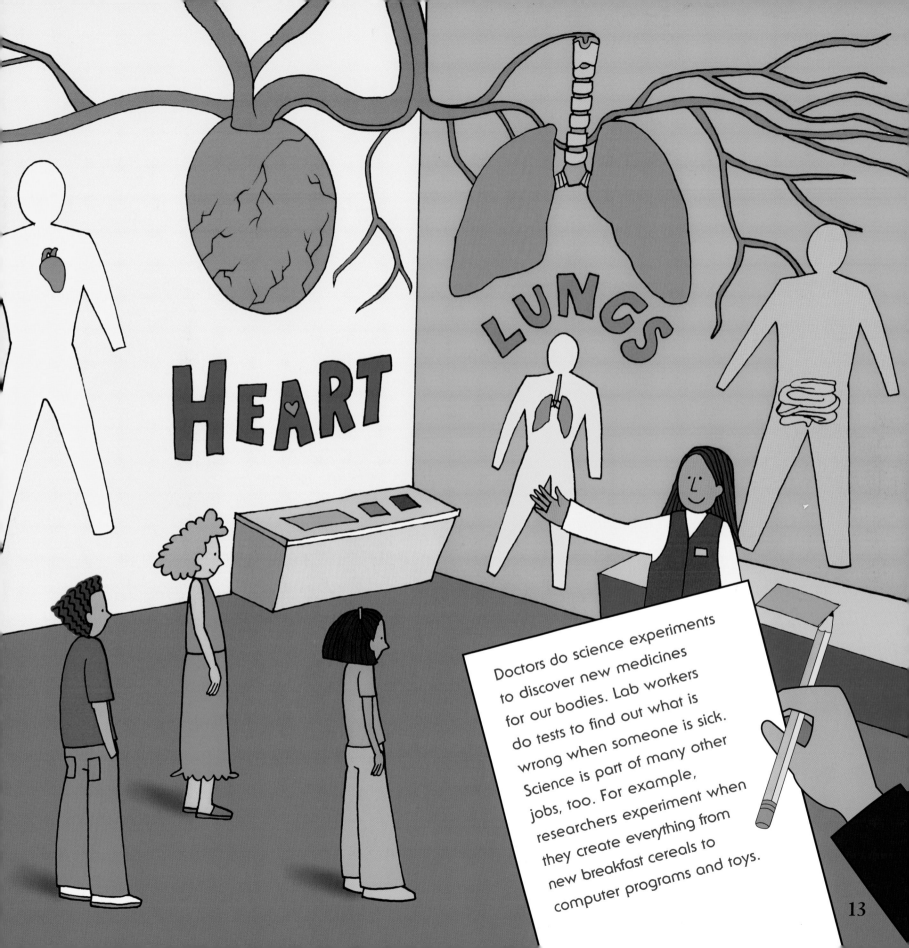

Doctors do science experiments to discover new medicines for our bodies. Lab workers do tests to find out what is wrong when someone is sick. Science is part of many other jobs, too. For example, researchers experiment when they create everything from new breakfast cereals to computer programs and toys.

HEART

LUNGS

13

In this area, you can use that smart brain of yours to solve problems and discover how things work. Make a simple machine, or design and launch a rocket. Build a house that will stand in an earthquake. Play with light, and make rainbows. This area has hundreds of activities.

SEE IT.
DO IT.

Some scientists study how people can use natural forces, such as electricity, magnetism, and gravity. Others study how we can use wind, water, and sunlight for power. Computer scientists have made our lives easier in many ways. They have even given us new games to play.

15

Now listen up, all you future space explorers! This is Maria at Mission Control. Study your math and science if you want to become astronauts. As you can see, it takes a lot of technology to launch a spacecraft. Technology is putting science to work to make things we can use.

Some science centers have planetariums. In a planetarium, pictures of outer space are shown on a large, domed ceiling in a dark room. Images of the sun, moon, planets, and stars are sprinkled across the dome. Visitors feel as if they are in outer space.

This theater has a giant screen where we show exciting films that explore our world. We might show a film about the highest mountain, a colorful coral reef, or playful dolphins. Are you ready to sit down? The movie will appear all around you.

Lower the lights!

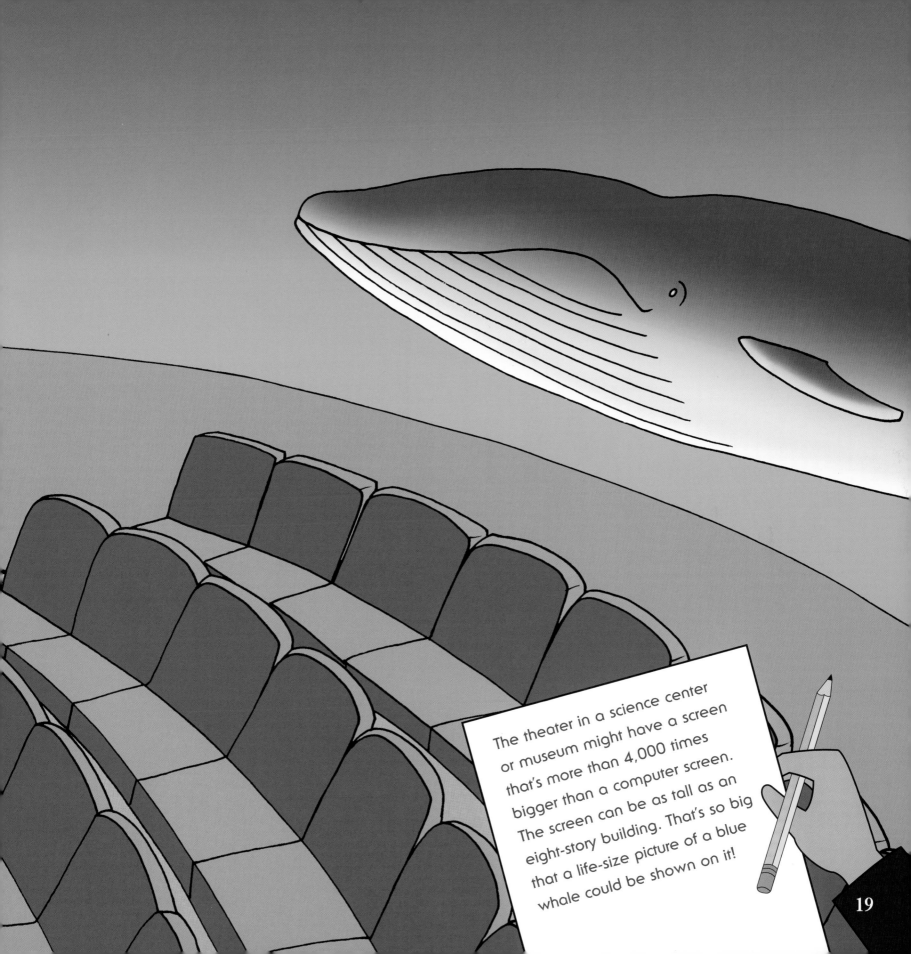

The theater in a science center or museum might have a screen that's more than 4,000 times bigger than a computer screen. The screen can be as tall as an eight-story building. That's so big that a life-size picture of a blue whale could be shown on it!

19

Thanks for coming to visit, boys and girls. I hope you got a sense of how amazing and fun science can be! Now you also know what a huge part science plays in our lives.

CREATE A SCIENCE MUSEUM EXHIBIT: FOSSIL DIG

What you need:

clay

small objects, such as macaroni
   in different shapes and paper clips

shoebox with lid

sand

marker

2 sheets of construction paper

tape

table for your exhibit

scissors

1 (or more) small paintbrush or makeup brush

1 (or more) pair of tweezers

What you do:

1. Form the clay into small dinosaur bones, teeth, or claws. Make other fossils by pressing the macaroni, paper clips, and other small objects into flat pieces of clay to make imprints. If you like, you can let the clay dry and harden.

2. Fill the shoebox with sand. Add your clay fossils to the box. Put the lid on the shoebox, and shake the box until all of the items are buried under sand. Remove the lid and set it aside.

3. Make a sign for your exhibit. Using a marker, write FOSSIL DIG in big letters on a sheet of construction paper. Hang up the sign with tape near your exhibit table.

4. Cut the other sheet of construction paper into smaller pieces about the size and shape of theater tickets. Write TICKET on each piece of paper.

5. Put the box with the sand and fossils on your exhibit table. Place the brush(es) and tweezers nearby.

6. Invite family and friends to visit your museum exhibit. Give each person a ticket. When a visitor comes to your exhibit, ask for his or her ticket and rip it in half.

7. Invite visitors to dig for buried fossils. Real scientists on digs are careful not to damage anything that might be buried. Instruct visitors to gently brush sand aside until they see an object and then to remove it with the tweezers.

8. When visitors have finished their digs, have them sort the fossils that are similar into piles. Can they guess what each fossil is?

FUN FACTS

- In the United States, all 50 states have science centers or museums. California has more than 30 science centers or museums!

- Science centers are for people of all ages. Some exhibits are more fun for younger visitors, and other exhibits are meant for older visitors.

- Every year, about 47 million schoolchildren around the world go on field trips to science museums or have museum programs at their schools.

- Exhibits and programs often differ from one science center to the next. For example, a center may or may not have a planetarium, a giant-screen theater, a space center, 3-D laser shows, an outdoor science park or playground, a discovery room, or a computer lab. One science center might have an exhibit showing live animals in their special habitats. Another might have an exhibit on ancient Egyptian mummies. Sometimes, science exhibits will travel from one museum or center to another. More than half of all science museums or centers offer overnights, or "camp-ins," for youth groups.

- The Museum of Science and Industry in Chicago, Illinois, is the largest science museum under one roof in North and South America. It has more than 800 exhibits and more than 2,000 hands-on activities.

GLOSSARY

cell—a basic part of an animal or plant that is so small you can't see it without a microscope

dig—the activity of carefully digging for very old objects that have been buried underground for years and years. A dig can also be the place where the digging is being done. Scientists might say they are "going on a dig" or they are "at a dig."

electricity—a natural force that can be used to make light and heat or to make machines work

exhibit—a display that usually includes objects and information to show and tell people about a certain subject

experiment—a scientific test to see what happens if you take a certain action

force—a power that can cause something else to move or change

fossil—the hardened remains or imprint in rock of an animal or a plant that lived thousands or millions of years ago

gravity—the natural force that pulls things toward Earth

laser—equipment that creates special beams of light. Lasers can create pictures of objects out of light that look as if they are the objects themselves.

magnetism—the natural force of a magnet, which pulls it to iron or steel

planetarium—a building or room that has special equipment for projecting pictures of the stars, planets, and other space objects and their movements onto a rounded ceiling, or dome

technology—the use of science to design and build something useful, such as computers

23

TO LEARN MORE

At the Library

Forbes, Evan, Janet Hale, and Cindy Christianson. *Simple Science Fun: Hands-On Science Made Easy*.
   Huntington Beach, Calif.: Teacher Created Materials, 1996.

Hauser, Jill Frankel. *Super Science Concoctions: 50 Mysterious Mixtures for Fabulous Fun*. Charlotte, Vt.:
   Williamson Publ., 1997.

Kohl, MaryAnn F. *Science Arts: Discovering Science Through Art Experiences*. Bellingham, Wash.:
   Bright Ring Pub., 1993.

Maynard, Chris. *Backyard Science*. New York: Dorling Kindersley Pub., 2001.

Murphy, Pat, Ellen Klages, Linda Shore, and the staff of the Exploratorium.
   *The Science Explorer Out and About: Fantastic Science Experiments Your
   Family Can Do Anywhere!* New York: Henry Holt, 1997.

On the Web

Fact Hound offers a safe, fun way to find Web sites related to this book.
All of the sites on Fact Hound have been researched by our staff.

1. Go to *http://www.facthound.com*
2. Type in this special code: 1404802975
3. Click on the FETCH IT button.

Your trusty Fact Hound will fetch the best sites for you!

INDEX